THE CARTOGRAPHER

poems by Robert Sargent

Forest Woods Media Productions Inc.
The Bunny and the Crocodile Press
Washington, D.C.

Library of Congress Card Number: 94-061028

International Standard Book Number: 0-938572-09-1

First edition printed 1994
Manufactured in the U.S.A.

Typography and cover design by
Cynthia Comitz, *In Support* Graphics

Printing by George Klear, *Printing Press Inc.*

Forest Woods Media Productions Inc.
4201 Massachusetts Avenue, N.W.
Suite 6061-W
Washington, D.C. 20016

To Grace Cavalieri
Poet and friend

PREFACE

The book is divided into two sections. The second section, *Now Is Always the Miraculous Time*, consists of poems first published in book form by The Washington Writers' Publishing House in 1977, and is published here by the kind consent of that publisher. Some of these poems had been previously published by various periodicals, as shown on the separate Acknowledgment page.

The first section, *Epiphanies, Small*, consists of later poems, and has its separate Acknowledgment page.

This book is made possible in part by the D.C. Commission on the Arts & Humanities and the National Endowment for the Arts. We are grateful for the support of these agencies.

INTRODUCTION

I undertake to introduce my friend's book a bit warily: how do I acknowledge that friendship (up-front as they say) and still say something which new and previous readers will not only find creditable, despite the implicit disclaimer, but useful as well. In short, how do I avoid making what I say sound like an abject blurb? It helps, if, as in this case, the friend's poems are the real thing, and if one has admired them and read them with pleasure for many years. And what is an introduction anyway but an occasion to say what one likes in a book, and to say it in a way one hopes readers will find interesting and persuasive? In the spirit of the above, fore-warning and all, I offer a few words about Robert Sargent's *The Cartographer.*

The book is in two parts, the first comprising a section of recent poems, the second a group of poems which includes nearly all of Sargent's first collection, a chapbook, now long out of print, entitled *Now Is Always the Miraculous Time.* And it is interesting to read the whole in this order: to read first the achieved positions, the evolved themes, of Sargent's most recent work. And then to read, in the second part, where Sargent began, to see that, thematically, the poems have moved, over the years to a more genial acceptance of the known world. And it is similarly engaging to trace the stylistic changes, to find, as in Stanley Kunitz's late maturity, that Sargent has come to a graceful relaxation of the line, along with a comfortable turning to the ever more colloquial and plain in his language.

In both parts Sargent is a patient and canny cartographer of our emotional world; and in poems both early and recent the miraculous is admitted, in both senses: that is, let in and confessed to. But, of the later poems, as perhaps indicated by its section title ("Epiphanies, Small") the thoughtful being who guides us has grown more respectful of the smaller revelations, and, by implication, more respectful of quotidian miracles. Sargent says as much in the title poem of the section:

> I look now for smaller epiphanies, those
> That reveal, not change, our lives.

It may be that the careful inversion in the section's title (with its comma's making a reflective pause) is itself a way to emphasize how some unexpected revelations are no less epiphanic (to this cartographer) for being ordinary.

But, however homely, these are discoveries that can sting. In "Sister and Brother," the sister (Winifred), speaking in old age with her brother, recalls with a pain sharply rendered, that, sixty or so years before, when their father had asked his son if his new wife was "*smart*," her brother replied, "'oh, she's about like Winifred'"; and the Winifred of the poem's present adds, "'Smart for a *girl* you meant.'" And despite a gesture of apology from her brother, she says, "'That's what both of you thought about Mother, too.'" She cries and dabs her eyes and says, "I've never forgotten that.'" It seems to me a real achievement to make so memorable a human in so few lines; Sargent does this often.

Other moments, if less poignant, are as modestly revelatory: in "Mimi At A Restaurant," a woman "90 at least," is patronized by the awkwardly extravagant compliment of a younger couple and takes its (and their) measure exactly. After the couple leave, so far from being moved or flattered, she says, "Well, isn't *that* ridiculous!" In "The Animals," after a number of original and apt reflections on the instinctual lives of animals, Sargent surprises and intrigues (this reader at least) by observing, casually, that humans too are called and driven as blindly as animals by powers beyond their reckoning. It sounds a little like the fatalism of Robert Frost: no sentimental illusions about free will.

The second section, as I've said, is not so much different thematically, as *prior*, as less evolved. Perhaps as a stylistic parallel, the section has an odd kind of formal currency at this moment in our poetry, as Sargent seems here either to have written out of an older tradition or to have anticipated by several years the return of rhyme and the fixed stanza, especially the quatrain. Mixed in with the free-verse poems he seems to have been writing at the same time, these are handled with eloquence and easy grace. The following is from "Forty Thousand Thousand Fathers":

> Behind us, forty thousand thousand fathers,
>   Who in their lust unthinkingly conveyed
> The little wet and chromosomal capsules,
>   From which we all incredibly are made.

There are several rhyming poems in the second section which show this sort of skill in the fixed metric. The poem quoted shows another side of the poet's intelligence: his bookishness and impressive learning, a philosophical side in quite clear contrast to the homelier poems (which I happen to prefer). In short, there are poems here for a variety of tastes.

What a poet's career Robert Sargent is having: an electrical engineer for nearly all of his professional life, before he retired (some twenty years ago) he turned more and more of his attention to his life-long loves, the reading and writing of poetry. Blessed with youthfulness (equally of mind, body and spirit), in the time since he turned his full attention to writing, Robert Sargent has published poems in more than fifty literary outlets, some of them our most distinguished journals and quarterlies (*Poetry Magazine* of Chicago, for example).

In addition, he has had work published in about twenty anthologies; and this will be his fifth book of poems. Such output has to be heartening for those among us who have, like

Sargent, done most or all of our publishing with small presses; and we all should be so productive in "retirement." May we also continue to be as intrigued as Robert Sargent by "the fascination of what's difficult," in Yeats's phrase, may we all strive as faithfully as he has for what Berryman called "that mysterious late excellence." And may we achieve it as often as Sargent does here.

The title poem for the collection depicts a twelve-year-old boy who has made a map of his neighborhood (prominently featuring, over-sized, his own house) and, finishing it, the boy finds it good: "as if he knew now finally where he was." Robert Sargent is too wise to make any such claim, but he has shown all of us (readers and poets) some engaging ways to chart the globe.

Roland Flint

CONTENTS

I. EPIPHANIES, SMALL

I.

EPIPHANIES, SMALL

ACKNOWLEDGMENTS – Section I.

The poems in this Section have appeared in the following publications: "The Concept of Force," *Songs from Unknown Worlds, Science 85*; "Hull and the Bard," *Ball State University Forum*; "Tom Ramsey" and "A Visit from Philip Larkin," *Pembroke Magazine*; "The Towers of Rosslyn," *Whose Woods These Are*; "Bones," "The Etruscan Sculpture," and "Mr. Buddy Bishop," *Hampden-Sydney Poetry Review*; "The Witch," *Cadelabrum* (British); "Lincoln Used Only One That," *New York Quarterly*; "The Heads," *Puerto del Sol*; "Old Billy," *St. Andrews Review* and *Only Morning in her Shoes* (anthology); "Sister and Brother," *Negative Capability*; "The Artists, Aging," *Nimrod*; "Epiphanies, Large and Small," *Kansas Quarterly*; "Heraclitus," *The Classical Outlook*; "Mr. Mencken," *Poetry East*.

HERACLITUS

He awoke one day at dawn on a high hill
overlooking the Aegean. Wine-dark it seemed, the sea,
restlessly moving, its surface flecked with white.
A fading star or two could still be seen,
and Venus, still effulgent. In the east,
the heralds of the sun, Aurora's rays,
were driving night away. Trees waved in the distance.
Far off, a cow bellowed its discontent.
Beneath him, he felt the hard and stony earth,
stubborn in its refractoriness. A town below,
small from where he saw it, began to wake,
smoke issued from its chimneys, figures emerged.
All these things, that day, somehow seemed one,
and subject to some question of importance,
one he'd been trying to put in words for days,
just below consciousness. Now they came to him,
on his high hill, that day, that dawn, that time:
What's all this stuff doing here?

THE VALEDICTORY

On the stage of a small high school there's a young man,
robed (it's graduation time),
before an audience of parents and fellow students. He's
small for his age, wears glasses, seems quite calm.
As valedictorian, he'll make the ritual speech.

He begins with a quotation from Samuel Johnson, speaking it
well,
about the uneasiness of doing something for the last time
(from the final *Idler*).
Seems an auspicious start.
Now he has launched into his memorized speech. "A feeling
not unmixed with melancholy," he says.
He embroiders on that for a while, then brings on Death,
"infallible, portentous, sure";
opines that thought of *it* will cow "even an idle and wastrel
spirit";
says the question "How have I used my time?" will bring
"foreboding to the hearts of all."

Then, on a rising note, "But there is a loftier truth," and
that, "though perfection is unattainable,"
"Each can do something, be it ever so slight."
At this point he forgets his lines.

After pausing an interminable time (it seems), he fishes from
beneath his robe a written copy, and resumes his theme
(later he'll be praised for his aplomb).
"Small kindnesses, a little love," and so forth,
until the end of what he's worked so hard on. Scattered
applause.

This was 1929, the words
from his adolescent script on a yellowing sheet,
        discovered recently.
And now, what about that young man, his speech, all that
        fustian?
I knew him well, once, or thought I did.
He's now a self so far away he seems another.
I think of him seventeen and trying.

THE RITE

What should we make of these two from the distant past,
A boy and a girl, so much engaged with each other,
Entwined on a living room couch?

What they were doing with quiet lips and hands
(Her mother known by them to be in the kitchen)
Was surely nothing exceptional.

The psycho-biologist says, “Some such behavior
As this is crucial for role development.” Adds,
“Without this, what we call stuntedness.”

All true enough. But a somewhat clinical view.
And the boy, old now, is instead caught up with remembering
The pigeons cooing outside,

The tiny beads of sweat on her upper lip,
The window, its tied-back curtains: things that were there
In that season of burgeoning time.

VIRTUES

Slowly they came to us, since we diverged
into our human pathway, and then put
some meaning in our jabber,

these notions of behavior, rooted in
old ways of ours conducive to survival,
validated by use,

contingent, surely, chosen by circumstance,
variable culture to culture, subject to change,
but once established, named,

in what seems now a noble elevation
from their mean starts, central to what we think
of others and ourselves,

and now that the gods have perished, all we have,
in our incertitude, to push us on
the way we want to go.

THE CARTOGRAPHER

A boy of twelve drawing a map of his neighborhood,
sitting at the dining room table, working from notes –
his paced-off measurements, the lines and angles.
No one has told him to do this. There's Cherry Street,
and up the hill, Shannon's Alley. Quinn's, too.
The vacant football lot across the street,
old Mrs. Grayson's house, set way back,
and in the other direction the tracks and viaduct.
A large square, labeled MY HOUSE, in the center.
Checking it over, he thought, it's all there,
as if he knew now finally where he was.

SISTER AND BROTHER

She'd had too much to drink, her words burst forth
as they sat outside together in the dark.

"Bob, do you remember – no, you wouldn't.
When you got married, that is, the first time,
the one you thought was secret but wasn't, the marriage,
Dad hadn't met your wife. And he was curious.
He wanted to know *one* thing. And he asked you
in front of me – I must have been 15 –
do you know what he asked you?" He was silent.
"No, you wouldn't." She swallowed some of her drink.

"Here's what he said. 'Robert, is she *smart*?'
Not is she nice, or loving, or made you happy.
Is she smart! Do you know what *you* said?
'Oh, she's about like Winifred,' you said.
About like *Winifred, me*! Dad knew what you meant,
and I did too. Smart for a *girl*, you meant."

She was crying, now, dabbing at her eyes.
She stopped, then said, "I've never forgotten that."
He squeezed her hand. "I was only 22," he said.
"I know," she managed to say. And then, slowly,
"That's what both of you thought about Mother, too."

After a silence, "My-on-naise," she said.
"Not may-on-naise but my-on-naise. *My*.
I always pronounce it that way. You can see why.
Out of respect for Mother. She called it that."

THE CRITICS

Two young men, book-charmed. Sprawled in their chairs
On the shady veranda, surrounded
By small town somnolence, cicadas humming,

One spoke in the yellow day of the long summer,
His voice resonant, low,
"None of them knew the color of the sky."

He held Crane's book, open at page one.
His narrowed Chinese eyes
Gave question to the previously held.

They mulled the phrase: a bookish thing to be settled,
Their opinions clarified.
The cicadas continued. The sun went down on their talking.

RITTER

Tall and bony, erect, Amerindian profile,
he'd greet us, striding into the dormitory room,
with "How!" his right arm extended, the palm forward.
Well-known on the campus, but only a few close friends.
We came together. I found he'd read the good books,
not the trash. Long discussions: Wolfe,
Hemingway, most of all Faulkner. After all,
didn't he come from just up Oxford way?
In the summer, thrown together by happy chance
in the same small town, the two of us learned the stars,
using the celestial globe we stole from the college.
We'd stand in a field south of town, peering up, pointing,
the night air delicious around us, the brilliant stars,
Vega, Altair, Rigel, sometimes a planet.
Whiskey a bond, drinking from the bottle together,
rotgut, we'd call it now, from Scrap the bootlegger.
"Boy, that's good!" we'd say, shuddering, gasping,
handing the bottle back.
Later, parted,
we corresponded for years. At first his letters,
intimate and fond, evoked our former closeness,
"Sargent," he'd write, "I'm sitting here at a table
way up in North Dakota. I got me a bottle.
Remember how you and I used to catch a frog
and scale that chainlink fence and put the frog
in the station box? To puzzle the station master?
I'm upping the bottle. 'Gu-guggle-guggle,' it says.
Wish you were here to help drink it." Stuff like that.

As time went on his letters dwindled in interest,
came less often, stopped, of course, at his death.
Years passed. These days I think of him less and less,
forgetting the books we'd discussed, the stars we'd found.
But once in a while something or other reminds me,
making me smile, of his old entrance, that "How!"
that arm extended, palm forward.

SIDNEY

The kind of man he was: we'd be driving along,
and a man driving a car in front of us
would accidentally kill his engine, stalling his car
and the line of cars behind him, including us.
They'd all start honking, except Sidney.
He'd turn to me and say, shaking his head,
"The poor son-of-a-bitch."

TOM RAMSEY

Friend and college roommate. Thin. Bespectacled.
What's left of him for me, an endearing memory,
is a small, silent gesture, a shake of his head
done for my eyes only, a powerful comment
on something pretentious we were listening to.
Let's say Al Brown was telling one of his lies
to a listening group. Or perhaps some visiting lecturer
spouting forth homilies, boring and platitudinous.
And Tom, let's say, across the room, listening.
When he could bear it no longer, he'd turn slowly
in my direction, give that small headshake,
to which I'd give a slight nod, in agreement.
What a meeting of what we thought superior minds!
This tableau, repeated, self-serving though it was,
gave us immense pleasure.
                                        Our paths diverged.
We didn't write, though still remaining friends.
He never got into poetry, I'm pretty sure,
nor had to listen to readings. Tonight, for instance,
if we were listening to some wordy poet,
were sitting across from each other, he'd catch my eye
for a long moment, then give that slight headshake.
I wish for that. And him.

OLD TOM EAKINS

Crossing the Schuylkill River, train or car,
I usually turn and look for John Biglin
in his racing shell below us in the river,
sculling away. No doubt timing himself.
Since I know little or nothing about boat racing,
it's somewhat surprising, this looking. And I don't know
John Biglin, either, though I know his look:
seated, leaning forward, in his shell,
grasping the oars firmly, his lean brown arms
ridged with muscle. Bandanna round his forehead.
But no use looking, he's been dead for years –
was painted in 1874 by Eakins
in this very river, and in this very pose.
This looking, then, must be for another reason:
I think it's something I do out of respect
for Old Tom Eakins, painting what he saw with exactitude,
showing us now, today, how it once was
in and about Philadelphia.

THE TOWERS OF ROSSLYN

There are those who sneer at our Mondrian fronts,
Deprecate our Euclidian austerity,
Affect to despise the glass and steel of our walls,
Cluck at our sheen,
And sigh for Victorian adornment, baroque fenestration,
In small-storied brick and stone.
But we say, fie on these shrills of parochial cant.
Give us a hundred years of ennobling time
To put on the aura of age,
And slowly we'll take on power and passion,
Relax into beauty, gain our adherents.
Picture the time of our dwindlement,
Only a few of us then left standing.
Then young women will chain themselves to our doors,
To save us from the wreckers' ball.

PLACEMENT

Thinking it important to keep in mind where I am
in this place and time, this earth, this century,
with respect to the historical spectacle stretching behind us,
at least that part of it drawn, graven, painted, sculpted,
as depicted on art cards, of which I have several thousand,
from the Aurignacian to Diebenkorn, arranged chronologically,
I turn to the stacks of them, count out a relative few
from where I left off yesterday,
and go through them one by one.

THE STUDIO IN AUGUST

Heat is descending on Old Town, Alexandria,
Going into the bricks,

Heating the air inside the uncooled building,
Infiltrating the room he calls a studio:

Only an inside door by which to enter,
One small window, high,

And it barred shut, a worn carpet,
A grocery box for a table,

But there is an easy chair, a fan,
Coffee by plugging it in,

A yellow pad for writing, a ballpoint pen.
Perhaps these will be enough.

THE ETRUSCAN SCULPTURE

Stands there, the enormously elongated human figure,
Stretched in its length, distorted, thin, towering,
The museum's pride. And we think

Of sorcerous conjuration, primordial fear,
Of powerful superstitions still extant,
Of magical tribal cults.

The Etruscan sculptor, however, out walking at dawn,
Had noticed his long shadow cast by the sun,
And thought, "That would make a good piece."

THE HEADS

They look like apples lying on the ground of a meadow,
from the distance, say, where the ring of soldiers is drawn,
but no, they are heads of men.
They are groaning, although the sun has not yet begun to scorch,
and the ants haven't arrived.
You will be wanting to know where this was and when;
then you could be angry at someone or something,
a man, a tribe, a country.
But what must be kept in mind, no distractions,
is what lies before us:
the soldiers there to prevent interference,
the heads, soon in the broiling sun. And the ants.

THE GIRAFFE

Beauty is pleasure regarded as the quality of a thing.
- Santayana, The Sense of Beauty

There is pleasure, over and over, in looking at the giraffe,
not the one in the Washington Zoo, nor in the jungles of Africa,
but the one on my desk, the sculptured work of an African artist,
the look of its body, its sloping slimness and grace,
the way it is poised on its long and tapering legs,
the black and brown mottled sides and back and rump,
the drooping thin tail,
but most of all the upreaching sinuous twist and curve of the
        stretched-up, extended neck,
which bears the small and delicate head, looking backward,
as if it were looking at me.

MIMI AT A RESTAURANT

A very old lady, 90 at least, in a wheelchair,
Sits at a table with two companions, younger.
Silent, her old eyes flicker.

A middle-aged couple, strangers, approach her table,
And one of them says, "Before leaving, we want to tell you
What a *beautiful* person you are."

Smiling, they leave, no doubt pleased with themselves.
The old woman looks after them, purses her lips, sniffs,
Says, "Well, isn't *that* ridiculous!"

OLD BILLY

Around the turn of the century, in Montana,
Two little girls would ride to school on horseback,
On one horse, I should add,

Named Old Billy, now too old for farm work.
They rode bareback, tethered Old Billy outside,
While school was going on.

When recess came, they'd go out with their lunchbags,
To find Old Billy resting, lying down,
Under a nearby tree,

His body providing a seat for the two of them,
While they ate their lunch. What one of them still remembers –
She's in her nineties now –

Is how Old Billy'd give a little sigh,
As they sat down on his rib cage. Clearer to her
Than the breakfast she'd had this morning.

MR. BUDDY BISHOP OF SALEM, VIRGINIA

Because when I called the motel the manager couldn't do it
herself, but knew someone who might, namely, you,
and when I asked you on the phone if you'd ship me the jacket
I'd left there, you said, "Sure,"
and when I said I'd mail you some money for shipping and
trouble, you said, "Wait till it gets there,"
and you said not to worry,
and because two days later the jacket arrived, neatly folded
and boxed,
I am reassured. Things are not so bad after all.

JAMES P. JOHNSON

A group of young people, in New York in the '40's
(the war had brought them together), went down to the Village
for jazz, and found him playing an upright piano
in a small, smoky night club. One of the group,
a Navy lieutenant, carried away by the music,
knowing the words to a tune Johnson was playing,
standing by the piano, began to sing, softly,
then with more confidence, under Johnson's smile,
swinging along. Those unerring chords! The timing!
At the conclusion, Johnson, a kind man,
said, "The lieutenant sings good."

The great jazz pianist surely, by next day,
was forgetting this small thing. The lieutenant, however,
still remembers it well.

MY FATHER AND RUSSIA

My father considered Russia an admirable state,
at least from about '31, when he got laid off.
He'd expound on this, sitting in the porch swing,
to me, a willing convert. "Now, Robert," he'd say,
fixing me with a stern gaze through his glasses,
"Listen to what Duranty says," waving the paper
(he subscribed to the New York Times). "Duranty says
the Russians are doing fine – they're putting in
collective farms in the Ukraine. Kicking out the kulaks!
Good riddance!" he added, grinning with satisfaction.
He felt, no doubt, a likeness between the kulaks
and those who'd laid him off, business men in Chicago.
It was easy, then, to approve of Russia. Duranty
and Anna Louise Strong were spinning their tales,
and there were our own delinquencies, men out of work,
hunger and hopelessness here.

Of course, in World War II, Russia our ally,
his approval deepened. Later, after the war,
when Churchill made his Iron Curtain speech,
he ridiculed it, and despite the cold war, through the '50's,
he never lost faith in that large and secretive country,
and went to his death that way,
like Hazlitt believing in France in spite of Napoleon:
both of them stubbornly holding their dream of a place
where people were treated fairly.

HULL AND THE BARD

Steeped in Shakespeare. Liked to quote him, too.
For instance, if some friend appeared decked out
in brand-new clothes, he'd look him over, intone,
"The glass of fashion and the mold of form!"
Or predicting how some ne'er-do-well would end:
"Himself the primrose path of dalliance treads."
Once in the lobby of an old hotel,
I was disconsolate over a current love,
and to cheer me up, he squeezed my arm and said,
"Sargent, listen. Listen to the Bard."
(We called each other by our last names then.)
He spoke slowly, savoring the moment, his eyes
crinkled behind his glasses: "Men have died
from time to time – and *worms* have eaten them –"
Pause. "But not for love."

That old affair worth only a smile, these days.
What seems important now isn't how I felt,
or even his sympathy, welcome though it was,
but the pleasure he took repeating Rosalind's lines.
Later he told me that what made them good
was that about the worms.

THE GENERAL

The general was an estimable man. We were together
in the bustle of Tokyo, 1961,
touring the streets in a staff car, remarking on people,
buildings, and so forth. The city was peaceful,
the people were smiling, the buildings were standing there.
My first visit. He'd been here once before,
in 1945, some distance up,
flying a B-29 from Iwo Jima.

We chatted amiably. Finally he said,
"It's remarkable! That they could rebuild it so!
After those miles of flames! I'd seen Germany,
it was nothing like this."
He looked at me with a headshake, frowning a little.
Since there was, on the one hand, his bravery, his care for his men,
    his love of his country, devotion to duty,
and, on the other, the charred Japanese,
what could be said? I liked the general.
I think I changed the subject.
We drove on.

THE CONCEPT OF FORCE

Found myself seated by chance a few years ago
at a luncheon for notables (I wasn't one),
next to Hans Bethe, the great German physicist.
I sat there, a layman in science,
trying to think of something to say,
and finally, after some awkwardness, managed a question:
"Dr. Bethe, in relativity theory – tell me,
has the concept of force between two bodies,
their mutual attraction, been superseded?
Do bodies behave as they do, coming together,
because space is as it is in the presence of bodies?
No force?" Dr. Bethe regarded me mildly –
he was a kind man, with a schoolteacher smile.
"Force," he said. "The concept of force.
Has it been superseded? I think no.
I think the concept of force will continue to be –"
he paused, as if searching for words –
"effective and useful." That was all.

I give you out there, for your mulling over,
the words of a great physicist,
"The concept of force will continue to be
effective and useful." Since this is a poem,
some of you doubtless will think I mean people,
when I say bodies, coming together,
and that *that* is what will never be superseded.
And that Dr. Bethe was put in the poem
to assist in the metaphor.
That is not what I mean. There is no metaphor.
I mean only what Dr. Bethe said to me, smiling –
– no more and no less –
about bodies in space and gravitational law.
Though of course you may think what you wish.

MR. MENCKEN

If I had been asked by Senator Robert Kennedy,
"Tell me about H. L. Mencken,"
as was Charlie Citrine, a person in *Humboldt's Gift*,
I would have said: "H. L. Mencken was the man who wrote
(referring to *Joan and Peter*, a novel by Wells):
"Nothing can exceed its laborious dullness, its flatulant fatuity,
        and its almost fabulous inconsequentiality,"
which, I think, would have conveyed some part
of the flavor of Mr. Mencken.

LOGAN'S SPEECH

John (or James) Logan (c. 1725 - 1790), Mingo orator

Logan's speech, delivered to Lord Dunsmore,
at once became well known. Cited by Jefferson.
What brought it on occurred at Willow Creek,
his family killed by those he thought were friends,
a band of marauding whites. The speech ended,
Who is there to mourn for Logan? Surely,
a long pause then. Silence. We can imagine
the speaker's stern brown face, the audience waiting.
Finally, two words: *Not one*.
                                        Afterwards,
Logan made war on the colonists, aided the British,
died a drunk. The speech, however, lived on.
At least the white man let the words be known
to his descendents, that is, till quite lately.
High school English fare, pre-World War II.
But now, I'm told by current English teachers,
no one has heard of Logan and his speech.
Presumably too rhetorical, too much feeling.
Consigned to where they keep "Abou Ben Adhem."
Not only these days none to mourn for Logan,
but few to mourn his speech.

A VISIT FROM PHILIP LARKIN

If he were here, brought back, and the two of us
were sitting in my living room, at ease,
surely the talk would turn to jazz and how
it seized us young. I'd tell him how my brother,
off at school, New Orleans in the 20's,
would bring home records he had learned to love,
Louie and his Hot Five. Stuff like that.
How once our father, lover of the classics,
came in our room, hearing "Skid-dat-de-dat,"
and said, disgustedly, "You call that music?"

Then Larkin, in his horn-rimmed glasses, bald
and smiling, in his proper British tones
would say how things once were with him, a boy:
"Louie, too, like you. 'Ain't Misbehaving'
was one of my earliest records, a great prize."
And then there were his student days at Oxford,
listening with his friends to Peewee Russell.
"You know, think how we're lucky, you and I,"
he'd say, "to be born in the very piece of time,
this century, I mean, when jazz came in,
and then the glory years, fifty or so.
We can be thankful for them."

"I've got a piece," I'd say, "a Condon group.
'How Come You Do Me Like You Do?' Wild Bill."
"Play it," he'd say, remembering but not sure.
I'd put it on, we'd listen, Ed Hall first,
two choruses after the Schroeder introduction,
and then Wild Bill, what we'd been waiting for:
first chorus sweet, restrained, his trumpet pleading,
and then the second, its sudden rambunctious explosion,

and the beautiful arabesques, descending chuckles.
He'd say, at the end, "Didn't hear Peewee." "No,"
I'd say. "Ed Hall and Hucko on this one.
Both good clarinetists, though." And he'd agree.

That's how the evening would go, old jazz records,
Teagarden, Ben, Spoon, Bean, Rabbit....
He'd have to leave. "Time's up," he'd say, smiling.
"I'm glad you played Big T. Ben, too, the best.
Maybe next time we'll get around to poetry."

SOCRATES

He is the ugly, baldheaded man with the big nose
In the streets of Athens, barefooted. Usually found
Exhorting the citizenry

With what seems a peculiar message: *the knowledge of good*
Is all that is needed to make for virtuous actions.
And indeed he does mean all.

He is famous for asking questions, pushing his auditors
Into reluctant agreement. Is held in respect
Both as man and philosopher,

But we have trouble with this, considering each.
There's his unfairness in argument (see *Protagoras*);
His obviously false modesty;

The serene belief he conveys in his own rightness.
And with respect to his teaching, we look back
On man's long record of shame,

On our rooted sinfulness, so deep, almost,
As to make us give up on us. Seemingly uncontrolled
By logic. How can we follow

His stubborn belief that men can attain salvation
By taking thought? Think of it, taking thought!
But now we see him more clearly

And begin to smile, as we think of him arguing there.
That pertinacious old man! Not for his remedies,
Rather his way of life,

For what we think he'd do, living today,
Our problems laid out before him. He'd mull our plight,
Grave though it surely is,

And always persistent, urbane, and humorous, smiling,
Intent on what is important, how we live,
Keep on asking his questions.

BONES

The lover feels his lady's skull,
The sockets for her lovely eyes,
Beneath the skin and tissue that
Will cover her until she dies.

Although he feels, he cannot see
What lies beneath his lady's skin.
It's just as well, he'd shudder at
The sight of what's concealed within.

When she's entombed, the steady course
Of rot will dissolution make
Of that concealing envelope
That chemic bondings make opaque.

But now the lover, snug above,
Forgetful we are all akin,
Is spared the implications of
Her toothy, skeletonic grin.

EPIPHANIES, LARGE AND SMALL

An epiphany Damascene! That's what I craved
once, to set me straight. A voice from heaven,
like that which Saul heard on the road –
he left Damascus Paul.

But that was then, and not surprisingly
it never happened, nor was ever likely.
I look now for smaller epiphanies, those
that reveal, not change our lives,

as when Jupiter told me last night, up there glittering,
"We're in this together, face it, both of us bound
to an insignificant star. Let's keep
things going as long as we can."

THE WITCH

There is a man removed, yet wound
    Deep in my web, who at demand
Of my soft signal gladly takes
    Himself in hand

For me. To exercise this thrall
    I call upon my wicked lore.
I do the trick with charming words
    Of letters four.

LINCOLN USED ONLY ONE THAT

That that? No, please! Only one that!
That that government should not perish, no!
That that, the second that, that is,
the adjectival that,
would mean a particular government, wouldn't it?
Lincoln meant something more general.
If he'd meant that, he'd have used this, not that.
That this. See?
One conjunctional that, one only, I beg of you.
That the type of government, get it,
of, by, and for the people
should not perish. See? One that.

THOUSANDS OF POETS

Thousands of new poets, writing, writing, working away,
a flood of poems and manuscripts overwhelming the editors,
nothing like it in history,
and the veteran poets, published more rarely now, go around
muttering, feeling aggrieved.
Fuck these veterans! Let them take their chances along with
the rest!
Let there be the young woman in Montana, painfully tapping on
a borrowed typewriter,
and the old man in Florida, working on his computer.

AN ARRANGEMENT OF WORDS

A Conrad Aiken character once said,
I think to a cabdriver,
– we can imagine a nighttime urban scene, a tipsy passenger –
"Take me to the number of numbers on the street of streets."
An ineffectual direction, surely. But
the brave arrangement of those dozen words! –
noble in their precise exclusiveness,
fit for his large desire,
and universal, too, for all of us,
naming a place where we'd all want to go.

THE SERIOUSNESS OF POETRY

One can play the fool everywhere else, but not in poetry.
- Montaigne, Essays, Book 2, Chapter 17

I will try to speak of the seriousness of poetry,
its exactions: how difficult it is
to write it clearly, without pretentiousness,
without vocal stumbling,
giving both sound and meaning their due;
to be considerate of readers,
to tell them enough but not too much;
to make sense,
but beneath the sense, something further;
to achieve the tone –
to build something that will stand there.

THE ANIMALS

The puma, his feral pounce, snarls of the wolf,
the waddling elephant's satisfied rumination,
each with its own performance,

the horse walking along, an occasional whinny
scaring the birds, not caring about his noise,
clomp, clomp, snort,

the cat rolling over on her back, sinuous, purring,
a soft meow now and then, sometimes a flash
of sudden and lashing claws,

beautifully apt behavior fit for occasion,
only concerned with what's close in space and time,
the road, these oats, this mouse,

the horse not thinking about what the other horse thinks,
and the cat not the cat down the road, the self uninvented,
suffering but not worrying,

imprisoned in their set ways, their roles laid out
by millions of years, but, like all of us, blindly
doing their best, trying.

WHEN

When in my slow decline I think of those
now gone, with all they knew of what I know,
how things went once, times past, now locked in me
for want of their sweet presence,

and some new thing comes up they'll never hear
to chuckle over, some new friend not meet,
then in this mulling over how things go,
there's fortunately you.

THE ARTISTS, AGING

Braque in his 80's, painting the dark subjects:
a huge black bird, such as a child might draw,
or a black weeding machine in an orange field,
a dark sky, the pigments rough, slashed on,
done as if not thinking but somehow knowing
from his long years,

and Hawkins, playing in the late 1950's,
Duke's tune, "In a Mellow Tone," and, his turn now,
the saxophone erupts with a brusque hardness,
an impatient honking, declamatory,
the almost dissonant notes unexpectedly placed
against the steadiness of the rhythm section,
twisting the tune his way,
what he now knew,

and Jeffers, his last years, I guess at Big Sur,
an old hawk now like those he loved,
the rough poems from deep sources, festering,
the angry words pouring out in unmetered lines,
mixed with love,
writing as he pleased, exactly.

II.

NOW IS ALWAYS THE MIRACULOUS TIME

ACKNOWLEDGMENTS – Section II.

The poems in this Section have appeared in the following publications: "New Albany, Mississippi," *Georgia Review*; "Mister Lester January," *California Quarterly*; "Jack the Ripper," *Poetry Northwest*; "The Torturer's Apprentice" and "The Beasts of Pitt Street," *The Lyric*; "An Occasional Man," *Woodwind*; "A Southern Poet," *Southern California Review*; "The Veterans" and "Questions for Myself," *Mississippi Review*; "Medusa," *Western Humanities Review*; "Forty Thousand Thousand Fathers," *Antioch Review*; "Eighteenth and K, Northwest" and "Rescue at Antietam," *Ball State University Forum*; "Gallery 35: The National," *The Washingtonian*; "A Young Couple, Seated in Front of Me, Before Curtain Time," *American Weave*; "For D. H. Lawrence," *Shenandoah*.

NOW IS ALWAYS THE MIRACULOUS TIME

Beneath noticing: there is Wyatt lying
Holed up in a London chamber, thinking of Anne,
And all the mice are frightened.

The Faulkner ne'er-do-well has taken a job
Wheeling coal at the power plant, late shift.
He scribbles from midnight to four.

And in Storyville or out at Lincoln Park,
When Bolden blows his raucous calling horn,
The boy Louis is listening.

NEW ALBANY, MISSISSIPPI

A crooked concrete road through slanted hills.
The stepchild state. My old stomping ground.
It slips up on a small one-storied town,
Whose dreamy people softly speak a tongue
Like mine, hence dear. And I always look for a sign
On the winding approaches, announcing the town's distinction.
Last time, again, they hadn't erected it yet.
After the foreign acclaim, the Swedish honor,
They didn't put up the sign; and when he died,
Still the old craftsman, joining words to insight,
No sign of a sign. There has been no discernible change.
But I think some day in the town's procession of days
The workmen will get their orders, the truck will be loaded,
And cars will parade behind to a suitable site,
For a suitable ceremony. Patience, now:
I'll be going back soon – when I do, I'll look for the sign.

A STUDENT AT ALEXANDRIA

I.

These thrown-up buildings, unrelieved by time,
Squat, ugly and raw in the dustiness
That clouds the parting sea.
                                        I think always
Of the Long Walls, of coolness in cobbled streets,
And a certain style in black-and-ocher vases.

II.

My father and my uncles used to talk,
Sipping the watered wine on quiet evenings,
Of the old days, when there were only Greece
And hinterland; when what barbarians did
Was no affair of ours, provided only
They stayed home. Days were Athenian,
Until the young upstart from Macedonia,
An outland Greek, discarded all the things
His tutor taught, and pushed us into Phrygia,
And on to Africa (where otherwise
I wouldn't be), and then on to the east,
Defeating Persia and the savage tribes
Of Asia till he got beyond the Indus.
And they all said he forced our Grecian world
Into a new world's chaos. I say only
Why did he have to leave us Alexandria?

III.

There came two soft and jeweled teen-age flirts,
From Corinth and from Thebes, competitive
To separate me from my patrimony.

Small things led up to large ones: reprimands
And family councils; finally, Athens barred,
And shipped protesting off to this raw town,
A sullen scholar, studying mathematics
Under the usual master. However, Euclid,
I must confess, compels a certain interest.

IV.

Of course, he is a Greek. We gather in
An inner court. We sit upon the ground.
Comes in, a bearded gray old man, quiet,
And greets us softly, with his eyes half-shut
To weigh our latencies, assess our minds
Against the rigors of his demonstrations.
He hopes for us. He teaches us straight lines
(While I am dreaming soft Corinthian curves)
And triangles. How that man loves triangles!
All figures are his love; to their design
He fits his gentle words – I think he thinks
Geometry made the world and antedates
The constitution of the sensible!
Somehow, I can't believe it made my world:
Horses and games, theater, wine, talk –
And sunrise for two in a green and chirping garden.

V.

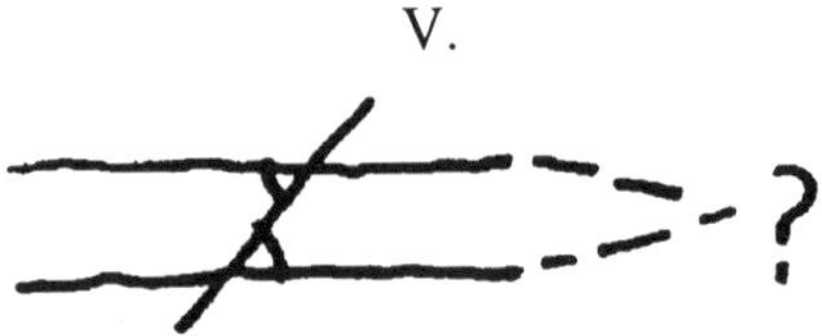

He draws three lines in the sand with a pointed stick,
One crossing the other two, slowly intones:
"Let the alternate angles be equal each to each.
Now I will show that these two lines can't meet."

(If my soft Theban friend lay parallel
And close to me, I think we'd surely meet.)
He starts his proof with the hypothesis,
And calls upon the Sixteenth Proposition,
Book One. Oh, what he needs, he remembers! Ends:
"Thus the lines can't meet, no matter how far extended."
No one disputes it. Silence. Above us, storks
Fly north, for a barbarous summer. Will he dismiss us?

VI.

No. He wants to discuss an additional point,
Having to do with the converse proposition:
The angles *not* equal: prove the lines will meet.
He speaks of "perverse plausibility," "fruitless approaches,"
And of adding a fifth postulation, as if he believes
Someone might care in a couple of thousand years.
There are cares and cares: this might be someone's care.
What I care for lies north across the sea,
And his reflective words cannot engage me.

VII.

He lets us go. I walk through unpaved streets.
There are ships from home at the newest dock. Would father
Allow a visit? No. I know no;
No use to ask, no use to think of asking;
I know, for now, I am beyond all asking;
And I curse this city and the founder of the city, him
Who ranged the world, left his name here and there,
And died some years ago in Babylon
Of a sunset fever, under an onyx sky.

FORTY THOUSAND THOUSAND FATHERS

Behind us, forty thousand thousand fathers,
    Who in their lust unthinkingly conveyed
The little wet and chromosomic capsules,
    From which we all incredibly are made,

Provide the serial suffering links, unbroken,
    Which, one by fateful one, from you and me,
Through naked, hairy, scaled and bony creatures,
    Lead finally to the warm Devonian sea,

And there we find our forty millionth father,
    All gilled and finned. His fishy, baleful eyes
Inform us that the piscine brain behind them
    Gives us no warmth with which to sympathize.

And forward? Do you think our aspirations,
    Puffed in the half-way house of earth's long run,
Will matter to that cold, bizarre descendent:
    Our alien forty thousandth thousandth son?

LONE HAWK, COMANCHE COUNTRY, 1700

Usually now I sit outside the tipi
Watching my old dog.

He used to pull the travois, many miles,
Over the level country.
They pull them now with horses.
I used to hunt the buffalo on foot,
Disguised a buffalo, creeping slowly up,
Freezing under their mild, incredulous stare.
That took some doing.
They hunt them now on horses.

Today my grandson tried to make me ride
His horse. Come on, he said, try it.
I looked him down with no.

My old dog, dreaming, chases a rabbit,
Whines, twitches his legs. I say yes,
Catch him! Eat him! Gobble him!

MISTER LESTER JANUARY

Mister Lester January, I never met you,
But forty years ago you were a butcher in Vicksburg,
And I saw your sign many times: Lester January, Butcher.

Mister Lester January (if you are still with us), you won't remember
You bought a little goat once, as a routine transaction,
Whose name was Mondamin. You couldn't have known his name.

Mister Lester January, Mondamin was my little goat.
Had a little "baa"; loved milk; and butted me gently.
Became a nuisance to parents. Had to be sold.
And you were the chosen recipient.

Mister Lester January, I am not angry, but one question, please:
That time when you butchered and sold Mondamin,
Tell me, did you describe him to customers truthfully?

THE VETERANS

Among the standing guests, his dark eyes roving
Over the fair green lawn, the wedding party,
Fitchett,
Loquacious salesman, brash,
Erstwhile radioman in an armored division
(Part of that lethal swarm tentacular
Known to all martial men as Patton's Third),
To whom time now had added twenty pounds,
Descried,
Great among guests,
A drink in hand, watching the chatting scene,
A burly affable man, his old commander
(But four-starred now, well-known as "General Abe"),
And thus to whom
Fitchett presented himself as an old buddy.

Both rising to the civil, soft occasion
As once to those brought on by arduous war,
The general first, polite in standard gruffness,
Guided by ancient and unwritten script,
Inquired his outfit.
The ascertainment of this vital datum
Gave them the proper start. Their roles now set,
Initial hours in Normandy were broached.
The beachhead and its tense beleaguerment,
The slow, precarious build-up, chancy once,
Were now, from twenty years and many miles,
Mere prelude to their triumph.
Verdun and Metz, surrender foreordained,
Fell to them as their due.
The anecdotal reminiscences
Of weather and terrain,

The quality of opposition arms,
And the always prime importance of supply
Were dealt with in a soldierly accord.

On the green lawn, ringed with its ivory dogwood,
The fair young bride, obedient to her role,
Cooed at the milling guests. The dialogue
Drew to its classic, precedented close.
The general had to go. He drained his glass.
"Well, good to see you, Fitchett." Jovial now,
Both smiling in the mutual evocation
Of an earlier, simpler time, a common past,
They parted to their futures. Straightening a little,
Sucking his belly in,
Fitchett marched off to make his au revoir.

GALLERY 35: THE NATIONAL

The Maid had bravely burned six years before,
Before her human judges. Times were poor.
And the cruel audacious wolves who softly crossed the frozen Seine
Ate children in the moony streets of Paris.
Famine visited prudent and careless.
Not much below but pain.
But the testament system was simple, not hard to explain,
And no questions were raised. All was clear.
Heaven was near.
And the Amiens artist was confident.

From Matthew's work he most respectfully
Derived his argument. The Virgin pregnant
And regnant in her shy serenity,
Stands swollen, to the fore. Joseph, behind the wall,
With down-turned mouth and dark suspicious frown
(He doesn't see the bright suspended crown),
Looks sulphurously forth at the Madonna.
Fortunately for all,
There is another, thoughtful for her honor:
The attesting angel puts his hands in hers,
And by this act avers
That Joseph errs.

The painter, doing for God the best he could,
Surely looked at his work and found it good.

MEDEA, AT THE KITCHEN SINK

Critics say
We are now bereft of the ancient symbols
(The sword, the throne, the Book)
That gave some elevation to our deeds.
For duels at dawn we substitute the lawsuit;
For the kingly curse, the prophet's anathema,
We trade mean gossip at the country club.
No dignity. No height.

But I know an admirable woman,
Can lift a sordid, ordinary quarrel
Up to a high Euripidean plane.
Consider how she shows her view of marriage
To that awed audience of one, her husband.
First, an expounding of her bitter heart
Against his lacks, in slowly rising tones
Of choice and masterly vituperation.
Now standing above the sink, she flicks the switch,
Starts the disposal running,
Pauses....

Then stripping the ring from her hand,
She hurls it down the gaping garbage hole!
The whir turns to a roar. Both of them know
That what goes spinning down the sucking drain
Is more than merely fragments.

In the noise of the grinding rasp that chews their troth,
She closes the scene suitably....
Fittingly....
(Aristotle would have approved)
Shouting obscenities.

THE BEASTS OF PITT STREET

I quit my paved and safe, my gardened court,
    My private fort,
And slink outside into the Pitt Street fog,
    But that wild dog,
Who bounding comes and snarling bounds his way,
    Brings me to bay,
And dodges, darts, evades the fatal bands
    Of my strong hands,
Till I devise my plot, lacking all mercy:
    I my own Circe
Become the crouching beast, sink into place.
    His lupine face
Droops at the threat of my most cruel lunge,
    The feral plunge;
He dwindles in his pensiveness; looks by
    My glistering eye
In his small cowedness. And not only he.
    I frighten me.

AN OCCASIONAL MAN

From time to time, there has been an occasional man
Killed by a bear.

We might think of one of these men.

A Kansas trapper, perhaps, in the early days.
A dry, hot day? Maybe hunting?
No, tending his traps. But certainly out to kill something.
Stuffing small rodents, mostly alive
(Although not for long), in his sack.
Was there a sign, perhaps unobserved, a warning?
Then a RUSH! and a great growling furriness
Over him, taking him, tearing him,
Crunching through his nice bones. Weakening screams.
Dismemberment there for a while.
Later,
The family would find a forearm here of the father,
And there his gnawed but delicate thigh bone.

The shambling bear
Would stretch to run from the dogs of the trailing hunters.
Caught up with, surrounded, would bat them away for a while,
Flipping them whining over,
Until the hunters arrived.

Later that day, the sun would go down as usual,
And slanty Antares comes up as usual red.

A SOUTHERN POET

"I do not know how many times Jordan shot.
Jordan then said, 'You didn't leave me anything
but a nigger, but at least I killed me a nigger'."
- Washington Post, October, 1967

"But at least I killed me a nigger."
How talented Southerners are in the use of poetry!
Notice how softly the opening anapest
Ascends to the strong spondee "I killed,"
And declines to an anapest tagged with a feminine ending.
Could Pope have done better?
And mastery of case! Flawless, the dative "me"
Next the accusative "nigger."
No doubt the craft unconsciously learned, drunk
From the jasmine air –
Boys whispering under a yellow streetlight –
His heritage.

MY OLD COMPANION

My old companion of the lawless days
Is now my errant sister. Who can say
Our self-torment did not deserve some praise,
The judgments of the uninvolved, a stay?
That both of us, within the somber maze,
Did not present our faces to the day?

MONODY FOR BOWIE

Developments initially were slow, but at the last
Came fast,
And Bowie died in the time of the stretched out year,
In the month of falling leaves.
Curling, withering, they finally fell from the tree.
So too he.

In better days, he was wise and kindly,
Easy to talk to, humorous, thoughtful for others,
Liked whiskey, talk – gregarious enough –
But sometimes chose to be alone (politely).
Had knowledge of the world, never a pedant,
And judged with wisdom where to draw the line
Between tolerance and indignation.
Differing, a smile.
Thus his style.

He cared for words, their sounds, their printed look,
Liked Thomas, Lawrence, Yeats,
But most of all loved Hopkins,
And in the season of the shortening day
Would sometimes read him from a blueish book
(His chair placed by the light from long glass windows);
Later,
As summer turned to fall and he in bed,
Ask he be read.

From the days of the slow terrible revelation,
All was kept locked, no burden shared.
At times one might have thought him unaware,
But for a certain intonation, tension,
When quoting certain lines:

"Do not go gentle into that good night,"
"How far from then forethought of,"
And a flash from calm eyes behind horn-rimmed glasses,
And a certain tilt to the head.
No more said.

Yet all was said. I wanted it otherwise:
Wanted a simple "I'm scared," so I could cry with him;
Wished that he had not earned, in the dying year,
Our gratitude
For fortitude.

QUESTIONS FOR MYSELF

If there could be
A replay of some old catastrophe,
A turnaround of some old gauche mistake
(The kind you make

When unaware),
And now it could be altered, rendered fair,
Made finally right: which would you finally choose,
Which ones excuse

From its repair?
The smile teased from you on the witness chair?
Your stumbling exit from the picture show
(The Alamo),

A refugee
Of twelve, fleeing the lovely Marjorie?
The bargain made upon the Harlem stair?
The boy Pierre?

Or possibly,
Having reviewed them all, you'd let them be
Unchanged in their old time, their Robert hour,
Their Sargent power?

NO SUN

Opening his eyes to the day's tribulations,
He slips from the bed, his side. Careful, no noise.
Performs his ablutions. Dresses.
Is he ready for the day? Anything noble today?

He heads for the kitchen, must have coffee.
But first the window for the first long stare.
There will be other stares on this long day.

This morning, no sun. From the window, clouds,
And down below the colorful cars
Skid on the icy road.

What can he make from this bleak scene?
Suppose a crash! Somebody hurt!
He sees his precipitous dash, ten stories down.
The bearded hero. Noble in that cold wind.
Quick in attendance. Gentle for suffering.
And modest under the merited accolades –
Almost humble.

Turning away, now for the coffee,
He can hear, from the bedroom, a soft moan,
Somebody in pain for the bearded hero to tend to.

DIDO, FROM THE SECOND CIRCLE

Mississippi? Yes, I once was there,
Some years ago, responding to a call:
"Help me!", the urgent kind,

As most of them are, all over. This young girl –
She didn't even know to whom she prayed,
Had never heard my name,

But the system works. Her call came straight to me,
A soft wild cry, from her hell down to mine.
Despair in Mississippi.

I know my duty and I came at once.
A high school picnic, near a rural town.
Teenagers horsing around.

I found her sitting in a lonesome car,
Parked on the other side of the wooden tables,
Alone, her bare brown legs

Crossed tensely tight, defiantly awaiting
A bitter confrontation, imminent,
With her Aeneas, who,

Bucolic in pimples, ambling unaware,
Pondering God knows what but not of her,
Blundered along near by.

Invisible, I quickly slipped beside her.
I made her feel me there. She felt me there.
She drew strength from my strength.

And when he came abreast and, startled, jumped,
Her spirit now was mine. And oh! the scorn,
The fierceness in the look

We gave to him through our undropping eyes!
He couldn't find the will to stare us back,
And turned rebuked away.

All over. Sadness, all. Of course she took
Some comfort from his rout. And I could smile
At the sameness of all of these scenes....

But smiles are for things outgrown. And that older scene
Is with me still – the Trojan ship's push-off,
And the final, vanishing sail.

MEDUSA

Medusa, old and reliable attestations agree
You were evil and imperious. They say your lidded look
Was all it took
To turn a man to stone.
No doubt your power has waned. Yet if to me
Your harlot eyes were turned in speculation,
Your voice a slurry moan,
At least one part
Of this soft flesh I live in (not my heart)
Would rise to meet your cruel contemplation.

RESCUE AT ANTIETAM

On this old ground
Of old blood, on a Wednesday afternoon,
They say a graysuit shrillybilly tune
I never heard (my grandma's brother's sound)
Was all played out, and Burnside's bluesuit men
Were finally Sharpsburg bound.
And they say then
The billowdust of A. P. Hill was seen
(He was coming up, coming up, hard!),
Then his red shirt! And the silvershiny sheen
Of that high sword
With which he'd whopped his men from Boteler's Ford
In a sweatstrain gaspy march! It saved old Lee.
His dying words were of that gallantry.

That war....
I get out of the car.
A fence, a road, markers, a gray sky....
A breeze they didn't have.

Now if I cry:
Avoid the attribution of the tears
To those old years,
Old fought, decided, brothers' battles. I
Am maybe wishing, for a later day,
Another rescue from another fray.

A FUNERAL AT CLARKSVILLE

The slow procession of cars turns in the gate,
Winding among the tombs.
Gently stops.

From a tree near by, a redbird is whistling.

The dressed-up people soberly get out.
They mingle together, chatting softly,
Decorous as the tended grass they stand on.
Everyone wants to be where he should be.
Slowly they walk to the canopy. Oh, a profusion
Of colorful flowers! Cards from the donors, too.

The family finds its way to the folding chairs.
They sit quietly.
Now the service begins.

Meanwhile, the redbird keeps whistling
From his tree, arrogant and plumed, whistling,
Whistling –
For other ears than theirs.

THE TORTURER'S APPRENTICE

Because he couldn't pluck a fingernail
        With tongs, at the first try,
And let the squirmy object's hopeless wail
        Weaken the red iron's fry,
He was booted out, fired. And so young! Whither his life?
And what in God's green world to tell his wife?

A YOUNG COUPLE, SEATED IN FRONT OF ME, BEFORE CURTAIN TIME

He speaks of those four knights who tempting came
To Becket from the king; the use of choruses;
What lay behind the king's presumptuous claim;
And the choice of rhyming verses.

And she listens. She listens well. Of course to learn –
But fondly too. She knows it is his hour
To teach as young men must. She knows her turn
Will come in its quiet power.

A SMALL ENCOUNTER

The hunting spider is moving along, spraddle-legged.
He is stalking a caterpillar. Bear in mind,
What will happen is usual.

The caterpillar inches forward. The spider pauses....
POUNCES! Bites! Squirts his venom.
The caterpillar stops moving.

Please, no revulsion. The spider is acting the spider
In his fierce world: surely he advances
The future of spiderdom.

And the poor soft worm: at least he is fortunate
That he didn't know till then the precariousness,
The built-in thinness of things.

JACK THE RIPPER

Trembling, in the fog, in the dark, in an East End alley,
    With his sharp knife,
He waits for small sounds, Sal's heels, Bett's cough, to sally!
    And add a life,
With the usual screams, to his set. All once can say
    For his dark ghost:
He must have felt the *strangeness* of women, their way,
    More than most.

EIGHTEENTH AND K, NORTHWEST

Over this parking lot, say fifty feet
Straight up, I used to couch for questions. No
Good answers, I recall. Old problem days.
And now, below,

I'm parked. And older. The building is gone, for sure.
And the doctor's dead. What's left is only in me.
If all those words had worked, things might have gone
Differently.

FOR D. H. LAWRENCE

Your communication came
As I sat outside in the fretful night of a feckless day. The flame
Of the moment warmed me, and I said,
"Lawrence, I hear you, I hear you!" turning my head
Upward, heavenward. Somehow, it didn't seem right,
Either for heaven or you ....Quietly, the night
Displayed her many alternatives....I finally chose
The low and scorpion spot where raging, red Antares
glows.

TRUTH IN A PARKED CAR

We sit here in a parked car late at night,
Facing the avenue and Mr. Henry's,
Talking poetry,

Fresh from a reading. Quoting certain lines.
Your long brown hair goes well with my white beard,
Contrasting suitably.

Trustingly, we hold each other's hand.
The occasion calls for a story. I think of one,
True, of course,

That has happened millions of times, like all true stories:
About my role as lover long ago
To the trusting girls.

Nothing physical – no, the verbal felicity.
Love by voice. I say: envision a scene
Much like tonight.

I am sitting with a young girl in a parked car.
We are holding hands. (You squeeze my hand, doubtless
Picturing it.)

There is a gibbous moon, a cicada or two,
A cool night breeze. I am quietly telling her
Beautiful things

She'd always thought were true about herself,
But never heard them said. No one has told her.
Think of it, no one!

No one has praised her patrician looks, her virtues,
Her popularity, the way she walks,
The magnet power

She has for brave young men, including me.
The way we think about her in our dreams.
The way she is.

She sighs, wants to agree, cannot agree –
Agrees. She will remember. Softly the words
Have worked their charm.

I stop. Of course I am thinking of that old time,
And you are thinking of me and that old time,
Reflecting,

And now you ask, knowing you know the answer,
But wanting to hear it: "Really were those things true?
Those things you said?"

I say: think of it true as the parked car
And the low whir of the cicadas, believe it true
As the gibbous moon

Shining its mottled patterns on the trees,
Believe it for both of us, sitting together here
On this occasion.

NOTES

NEW ALBANY, MISSISSIPPI

Birthplace of William Faulkner

A STUDENT AT ALEXANDRIA

Aristotle, Alexander the Great's tutor, was rather narrowly pro-Greek in his viewpoint. See Enc. Brit.

The mathematical lesson Euclid is teaching the class is his Proposition 27, Book I. The converse proposition, which he says he is unable to prove, is his famous Fifth Postulation, unquestioned until the 19th century, when Gauss, Bolyai, Lobachevsky and Riemann discovered and developed "non-Euclidian" geometries. The version developed by Riemann was necessary to Einstein in his general theory of relativity. So obviously someone did care in a couple of thousand years.

LONE HAWK, COMANCHE COUNTRY, 1700

The Comanches were mounted by 1700 (Walter Prescott Webb).

DIDO, FROM THE SECOND CIRCLE

Dante places Dido here (Inferno, Canto V)

RESCUE AT ANTIETAM

On his death-bed, while in a coma, General Lee muttered, "Tell A. P. Hill he *must* come up!" (Douglas Southall Freeman)

The cover design is taken from a sketch of the author's childhood home in Vicksburg, Mississippi.